THE AMERICAN DREAM

J.W. Dicks & James L. Paris

Crown Oak Publishing●Longwood, FL

Published by Crown Oak Publishing
520 Crown Oak Centre Drive
Longwood, Florida 32750

Designed and Manufactured
in the United States of America

Library of Congress Cataloging in Publication Data

Dicks, J.W. (Jack William)
The American Dream:
The Ten Power Principles for
Financial Freedom
J.W. Dicks & James L. Paris
p.   cm.
1. Finance, Personal. 2. Financial Security I.
HG179.D53 1992

332.024-dc20   92-25907
                    CIP

ISBN 1-881209-00-8

DEDICATION

To the women in my life who make the quest for the American Dream worthwhile . . . my mother, my grandmother, my Aunt Pearl, my Aunt Jerry, my mother-in-law Dorothy, my wife Linda, and my daughters, Jennifer and Lindsay.

J.W.

To my wife, Ann, who has always believed in my dreams and helped me make them a reality.

Jim

CONTENTS

PAGE

PREFACE

The purpose of this book is simple--to spread the principles of financial success.

Americans are the essence of capitalism and free enterprise, yet we do not always prosper. We live in a land of riches, yet wealth escapes many. We questioned, "Why is that?"

Financial success is not difficult. Much of it comes from common sense. Unfortunately, this is not common knowledge, and that is why this book was written.

Give a man a fish and you feed him for a day. Teach a man to fish and you feed him for a lifetime.

Please, learn to fish with us....

INTRODUCTION

If you were to believe everything you hear on the news or what you read in the newspaper, you would be left with the feeling that the American Dream is dead. The negative speakers would prefer you to be left with the uncomfortable thought that things are going from bad to worse, and that your only choice is to tune in to tomorrow's news to hear how things have worsened.

Ladies and Gentlemen:

NOTHING COULD BE FURTHER FROM THE TRUTH. THE TRUTH IS THAT THE AMERICAN DREAM IS ALIVE AND WELL AND YOURS FOR THE TAKING.

Notice two things about the statement we just made.

1. The American Dream is alive.

By this, we mean that people do still dream the dream that made this country a success. Home, family, property, and success are still things cherished by most of us.

2. It is yours for the taking.

Note that we didn't say *asking*; we said *taking*. The dream was never available to people who did nothing to pursue the dream. It always belonged to those who reached out for the brass ring. Understand also that we don't use the word *take* in the context of "take away," but rather as to "step forward and accept the gift that is yours."

The purpose of this book is to lay before you the 10 principles of proven success. This is not some pie-in-the-sky gobblygook--these are the principles that govern success and will help you reach your own potential and gain your own dream.

This book is intentionally short. Ninety-five percent of all books purchased are never read because most people don't have the time. We have condensed everything with that in mind. We have made the point simple and have given you only the facts (as *Dragnet's* Jack Webb would have wanted). For those of you who would like additional information on the topics we discuss, we give you various recommendations for future study.

We have illustrated it to make it easier to understand. Mental pictures help both learning and retention. In this case, we wanted both.

Finally, we have put everything that is here on paper also on cassette tape because we know that some people learn better by hearing. If you have only the written version, you can contact us about the cassette tape version and use it for constant reinforcement.

For information, call toll-free 1-800-333-3700.

Within these pages are the building blocks for your American Dream.   In the beginning, the dream is fragile, so handle it carefully. After you have laid the foundation for your dream, have comfort knowing that all that is necessary to make it yours is to keep stacking the blocks.

A Summary of the 10 Power Principles for Financial Success

The Power Principle of Goals

The Power Principle of Time

The Power Principle of Credit

The Power Principle of Home Ownership

The Power Principle of Tax Reduction

The Power Principle of Money Management

The Power Principle of Protection

The Power Principle of Investing

The Power Principle of Work

The Power Principle of Personal Independence

STATEMENTS OF TRUTH

The Power Principle of Goals

Set out a road map for your life so that each day has meaning and each task accomplished helps you reach your ultimate objective.

The Power Principle of Time

Time is the one commodity that we have in limited amounts. We must use it wisely toward the fulfillment of our purpose.

The Power Principle of Credit

Credit, like money, is neither good nor bad; it is the use that makes it so.

The Power Principle of Home Ownership

Nothing exemplifies the American Dream like home ownership. It is our security blanket in life.

The Power Principle of Tax Reduction

Taxes can be a burden if we don't understand the process. We can choose to let someone tell us how to use our money, or we can take control of our own destiny.

The Power Principle of Money Management

Money is not the root of all evil. Money is simply a medium of exchange that allows us to move toward our goals.

The Power Principle of Protection

Protecting your family and your belongings is an instinct from birth. Understanding the modern tools equips you with the right instruments of protection.

The Power Principle of Investing

Even animals of the world set aside something for the future. We must follow nature's lead or be faced with lean winters.

The Power Principle of Work

It is a man's lot in life to work, but he is free to smile while he does it.

The Power Principle of Personal Independence

In this country, personal independence has been equated with retirement and financial stability. It has been viewed as the ultimate goal. Like all goals, you are the one who determines if it is bitter or sweet.

PART I

THE

POWER PRINCIPLES

PRINCIPLE 1

THE POWER PRINCIPLE OF GOALS

Goals are probably one of the most talked about subjects but unfortunately the least acted upon. A recent survey revealed the startling fact that the average American family spends more time each year planning their vacation than planning their finances. Many of the most celebrated motivational authors of the past 30 years, including Zig Ziglar, Dr. David Schwartz, and W. Clement Stone, have all positioned goal setting as a foundation for success. Even the Bible says, "People without a vision will perish."

So Why Are Goals So Important?

Over 85 percent of Americans retiring are dependent on family, charity, and Social Security as their only financial resources. Considering the fact that the average monthly benefit for Social Security recipients over age 65 is less than five hundred and fifty dollars, it means that the average retired individual either lives below poverty level or is a heavy financial burden on his or her family or society in general. Does this sound like a gloomy outlook? It doesn't have to be this way for you.

The Basics of Goal Setting

The simplicity of goal setting may be the reason that most people do not apply the Power Principle of Goals to their life. After all, how could something so simple be so powerful? The best definition I have heard over the years for a goal is "a dream with a deadline."

The Four Power Principles of Financial Goal Setting:

1. It Must Be Realistic

2. It Must Be Measurable

3. It Must Have a Deadline

4. It Must Be Your Goal

It Must Be Realistic

One sure way to develop a negative attitude about goals is to set unrealistic goals. Many Americans are guilty of this. It is known as the "get rich quick" philosophy. Rather than saving our money diligently over a period of years and investing it wisely, we want it all now. This mentality lends itself well to speculative investing, gambling, and a myriad of other investment pitfalls. Be realistic with your goals. Dream big, but be pragmatic.

A realistic goal: an achievement that can be accomplished with a reasonable plan

It Must Be Measurable

A client of ours, when asked what his financial goal was, replied, "I want to be rich!" We asked him, "What is rich?" He replied, "You know, I've never thought about it." Goals must be measurable! If your goals are "I want to be successful" or "I want more out of life," you do not have measurable goals. Measurable goals could include "I want a million dollars" or "I want to become chairman of my department," etc. Are you starting to get the picture? The lack of a specific target is one guaranteed way not to become a financial achiever.

It Must Have a Deadline

Remember, a goal is a "dream with a deadline." Why must a goal have a deadline? Without a deadline there is no possible way to devise a strategic plan to reach your goal. Let's take a look at a couple of examples of goals and how they can be easily achieved.

Goal Setter: Don Nelson

Goal: To purchase, within five years, a sailboat that costs $18,000.

Don is assuming that he can earn 12% on his money and has determined through the use of a financial calculator that he will need to save $220 a month. Don has decided to start a part-time business that should provide an additional fifty to sixty dollars per week to save for this goal. With this type of specific plan, Don will reach his goal. Imagine Don's chances of success if he simply said, "It would be nice to have a boat someday."

Goal Setter: Elaine Johnson

Goal: To send her son to college when he reaches 18. She anticipates the cost of a college education to be $20,000 per year, so she needs a total of $80,000. Her son is now eight.

Elaine assumes that she can earn 15% on her savings, and through the use of a financial calculator she has determined she will need to save $290 per month for ten years. Elaine has consequently started to work five hours overtime per week to produce the $290 per month. She has a definite plan and a definite deadline. How would Elaine's son have fared if she had said, "Someday I would like my son to get a good education"?

Goal Setter: Steve Miller

Goal: To accumulate one million dollars by the time he retires in 40 years.

Steve assumes he can earn 15% on his savings, and through the use of a financial calculator he has determined he will need to save $32 per month. Steve determined that he could easily save this amount by cutting down on his entertainment expenses. Steve never realized how easy it would be to reach his goal of becoming a millionaire.

It Must Be Your Goal

Goal setting is a highly personal exercise. Many families have group goals, and married couples also have shared goals. Remember, however, that in order to have the perseverance to reach your goals, they must be your goals. If you are not sold on the benefits of a goal that you have set, then you are probably better off to get rid of the goal now, because it is unlikely you will ever reach it. Take a long walk or spend some time alone and ask yourself what you want to accomplish financially. And, most importantly, write it down and create a plan to reach it.

Goal setting is undoubtedly one of the most powerful forces available to ensure that you will live the American Dream. The next time you hear someone say, "Someday I would like to have something," you may want to share this Power Principle with him or her, for it will most certainly change their life as it has ours.

"Goal setting is undoubtedly one of the most powerful forces available to ensure that you will live the American Dream."   *--J.W. Dicks*

Take a moment to do what very few people have ever done. List both your dreams and your goals. Your dreams are anything you would you like to have or do if you had all the money and all the time to do it. Interestingly, you may be pleasantly surprised that all these things that you want are really obtainable.

MY DREAMS

1. _____

2. _____

3. _____

4. _____

5. _____

6. _____

7. _____

8. _____

9. _____

10. _____

What are your goals? What do you want out of life? Write them down and make them a part of your daily thoughts. Your goals may or may not be the same as your dreams. Goals are usually more achievement oriented. However, your dreams can become goals.

MY GOALS

1. _____

2. _____

3. _____

4. _____

5. _____

6. _____

7. _____

8. _____

9. _____

10. _____

Now that you have taken serious time to list what you want out of life, make the time worthwhile by making these two lists a part of your life. As you make future plans and decisions, do so with these lists in mind.

PRINCIPLE 2

THE POWER PRINCIPLE OF TIME

"T-I-M-E, it's on our side. Yes it is!"
Mick Jagger, The Rolling Stones

Time can work for you or against you. It is either friend or foe. The choice is yours.

Each of us is given only so much time here on Earth to accomplish our task, and there is nothing we can do to get an extension. Consequently, the sooner we master time to our advantage, the more we will get out of life.

The Four Principles of Time That We Need to Master Are:

1. Compound Interest

2. The Rule of 72

3. The 10% Solution

4. The Law of Time Change

Compound Interest

There is only one part left out of Mick Jagger's famous song lyrics. Time is on our side, "if we use it." Maybe the better way of saying it would be *"use it or lose it."*

The sooner you learn to use time and its elements to your advantage, the faster you will accomplish your goals.

For example, $100 per month doesn't seem to be very much money and would hardly seem enough to supply an adequate retirement program.

Yet $100 per month invested at 12% will compound to $189,863 after 25 years and will grow to an amazing $649,626 after 35 years.

Better yet, if you can increase your interest rate to 15% per year, the same $100 per month will grow to $1,486,164 after the same 35 years. The table below shows you the growth of $100 per month at various rates of return and over certain year periods.

	10th Year	20th Year	25th Year	35th Year
8%	$18,516	$59,394	$95,836	$231,017
12%	23,333	100,014	189,863	649,626
15%	27,965	151,695	328,507	1,486,164
18%	33,725	234,448	582,431	3,509,848
20%	38,336	316,247	862,770	6,308,447
22%	43,686	429,294	1,287,658	11,434,694
25%	53,380	686,009	2,375,594	28,258,963

From the above table, you can see that the American Dream of becoming a millionaire is not outside the reach of anyone. And that means you. People willing to follow a consistent savings plan over their lifetime will retire with all the money they will ever need. The key is to start as soon as you can, using time to your advantage.

The Rule of 72

The Rule of 72 is a quick way to remember the number of years it takes your money to double--based on a certain yield or return.

This rule is important because it helps you to make investment decisions fast.

For example, assume one of your goals is to buy a house and that it will take $20,000 for a down payment. You have $10,000. You want to buy the house in less than five years. Right now, your $10,000 is in a money market account earning 6%. Do you have a problem?

The Rule of 72 can be quickly applied to help you. To use the rule, simply take the number 72 and divide it by the percentage of interest you are earning on your investment. The answer is the number of years it will take for your money to double.

Yield	6%	12%	15%	20%

Years to Double	$72 \div 6 = 12$	$72 \div 12 = 6$	$72 \div 15 = 4.8$	$72 \div 20 = 3.6$

This rule illustrates the importance of not accepting a yield on your investment lower than what you need in order to reach your goals. Remember, in our illustration we had $10,000 earning 6% interest, and we needed it to double in five years. Unfortunately, $72 \div 6 = 12$ years.

Consequently, to reach our goal within our given time, we must somehow increase our return.

Investment time can work for you or against you. Knowing the rules will help you to quickly make investment decisions.

The 10% Solution

The 10% Solution is a savings system. The concept comes from Biblical times, when people were taught to take 10% of what they earned and save for their future. No, this isn't the same as the tithe; this money is your savings.

If you are like many people whom we tell about this magical plan, you have probably thought to yourself "But I can't save 10% of the money I make. I don't have enough money now."

If you say that now, you will also be saying that for the rest of your life unless you change your belief. At some point you must simply do it, and we are suggesting that it be now.

The other thought that people have is "How can 10% of what I make possibly be enough?"

The answer requires a little faith. It just is. You won't be able to retire tomorrow, nor will you acquire quick riches, but this is a definite path to financial success that everyone can follow because it doesn't require you to try to make extra money. The only thing required is the discipline to set aside 10% of whatever you get.

Let me show you a quick illustration.

You're 25 years old and make $12,000 per year. Retiring rich on the American Dream seems like a pipe dream. Fortunately, one day you read a book that tells you to save 10% of what you make. Well, assuming you never get a raise, $12,000 x 10% = $1,200, or $100 per month.

How much will you save by the time you are 60?

Return	35 Years to Go
10%	$ 382,927
12%	$ 649,626
15%	$1,486,164

Let me rephrase the question. How much would that little old $100 per month become by the time you are 60 and start thinking about retirement? A lot of money, right?

Remember, though, the key is to start. How about now?

The Law of Time Change

This principle tells us that the one constant to life is change. There is a season for everything, and everything has a season.

Knowing this tells you that in good times you must prepare for lean times. If you are in lean times now, just realize that it is only a matter of time before this too shall pass. Please understand that we are not promoting a theory that all things come to him who stands and waits, because if you do, you'll probably get left by the bus.

What we are saying is that there are cycles to business, investments, and life. Nothing remains constant, and you must be aware of change.

Based on this theory, we would understand that there are no good long-term investments. Stocks will rise and fall and rise again. Real estate will be one great investment at one point and a disaster at another.

Our quest for the American Dream must be made with our eyes open, ready to shift our focus based upon change that might prove

either disastrous or prosperous. If we watch for the change, we can
flow with the tide.

***

"There is an appointed time for everything;
and there is a time for every event under heaven--

A time to give birth; and a time to die;
A time to plant and a time to uproot what is planted.
A time to kill and a time to heal;
A time to tear down and a time to build up.
A time to weep; and a time to laugh;
A time to mourn; and a time to dance.
A time to throw stones; and a time to gather stones;
A time to embrace; and a time to shun embracing.
A time to search; and a time to give up as lost;
A time to keep; and a time to throw away.
A time to tear apart; and a time to sew together;
A time to be silent; and a time to speak.
A time to love; and a time to hate;
A time for war; and a time for peace."

--The Bible

PRINCIPLE 3

THE POWER PRINCIPLE OF CREDIT

Credit can be one of the most powerful wealth-building tools you can use, and it can cause financial ruin if not used properly. Our country is now recognized for two distinct financial hallmarks. Americans are the most leveraged people in the world, and we save the least amount of our income. Even our own government has become overwhelmed with debt. Rarely does a political debate go by without our national debt being the central issue. But is credit bad in and of itself? Absolutely not. The use of credit does, however, carry with it a great degree of responsibility.

The Four Power Principles of Credit Are:

1. Develop a Credit Plan

2. Clean Up Your Credit History

3. Establish Good Credit

4. Use Credit Wisely

Develop a Credit Plan

Our first principle of success involved planning your goals. Included in that process should be your own credit plan.

Very few people have thought about actually having a credit plan or philosophy. Yet the one they practiced without realizing it was a combination of "shop till you drop" and "buy now, pay later." The result is a debt burden in our society that saddles both individuals and our government. And we are now faced with the debt of the previous free-spending generations who took their credit for granted.

A credit plan is a purpose statement of how you will use the tool of credit to achieve your goals.

As we said, one credit plan is "shop till you drop."

Another, more appropriate plan would be that "credit will be used only toward reaching a life goal." Thus, if this was your credit plan, using credit to buy a house would be wise if home ownership was one of your life's goals. Using credit to start a business would be consistent with your goal of going into business for yourself.

Using credit to buy jewelry would not be following a credit plan unless acquiring jewelry happened to be your life goal.

Credit planning, like goal setting, helps you develop advance responses to those point-of-purchase impulses that tend to drive our decision-making processes. If the purchase is not part of your plan, it can't be made with credit.

Clean Up Your Credit History

If you are one of the unfortunate millions who haven't used credit planning, you may have developed a poor credit history. Unfortunately, this type of record will keep you from reaching your bigger goals. Poor credit history may keep you from buying your home, starting a business, or even getting a new job, since some employers use your credit history as an indication of stability.

The first and foremost action to take to get control of your credit rating is to get a copy of your credit report. This can be accomplished much more easily than you think. As a matter of fact, the Fair Credit Reporting Act entitles you to a free copy of your credit report if you have been denied credit. If you have not been denied credit, a fifteen-to-twenty-dollar charge is required. To find the credit bureaus in your area, look in the yellow pages under "Credit Bureaus" or "Credit Reporting Agencies."

Establish Good Credit

Trying to create good credit forces you to ask the age-old question: Which came first, the chicken or the egg?

How do you get credit without a good credit report, and how do you get a good credit report without first getting credit?

If you have no credit history, an easy way to start building one is with a secured credit card. A secured credit card requires that an individual make a deposit equal to the amount of available credit line issued on a bank credit card account. These credit cards look exactly like your regular credit cards and will show up on your credit file as positive credit once you start using them.

The following are two banks that offer secured credit card programs. Call to get an application form.

· Savings Industrial Bank   1-800-779-8472
· First Consumers   1-800-876-3262

Use Credit Wisely

We do not believe that credit itself is bad. It is the improper use of credit or becoming a slave to credit that is bad. Let's look at the four major areas of credit and see how they can be altered to develop a better credit plan.

Credit Cards or Consumer Credit

This type of debt is the most abused. Intelligent people who would laugh at the suggestion of borrowing money at 18%-21% do exactly that each month when they charge on their credit card and don't pay it off.

If you do nothing else with your credit but this, at least shop around for a better interest rate on your credit card. You can get rates as low as 8% (Arkansas Federal Savings, call (501) 227-5654: currently the nation's lowest).

Look at the difference between an 8% credit card and a 21% card on a $3,000 balance.

Balance	Interest Rate	Monthly Payment
$3,000	21%	$135.83
	8%	103.33

Monthly Savings: $32.50

What do you do with the savings? Use it to start the 10% Solution, of course. (See Chapter 2.)

Automobile Loans

The prices of new cars are spiraling upward. Sticker shock is now a normal result of any visit to a dealer showroom. Nevertheless, Americans need and want their cars. Here are some practical tips on auto credit.

1. **Shop rates**. Your dealer may make financing easier, but his rates frequently run higher. Car dealers now make more money on financing and credit insurance (which you should never get because it's too expensive) than they do on auto sales.

2. **The best loan is a three-year car loan.** The lenders would prefer you to take a four- or five-year deal. However, if you do, you'll just pay more interest the other years.

3. **You'll get a better deal on a car that is a year or two old.** No, not on the financing, but you'll save a great deal of money if you aren't the first guy to drive the car off the lot. Slightly used automobiles provide big savings.

4. **Don't buy the dealer's extended warranties.** In 90% of the cases, these turn out to be bad arrangements. Extended warranties cover items that normally don't wear out, and when they do, the company insuring the warranty is usually out of business or you have already traded your car.

Mortgage Financing

If any one item typifies the American Dream, it is home ownership. 99% of people finance their homes. Like all areas of finance, you can save big money by understanding a few easy principles.

1. The two major types of mortgages today are fixed rate and adjustable or variable rate. A fixed rate mortgage "fixes" your interest rate at a certain amount over the entire term of your mortgage. A variable rate mortgage allows the interest rates to fluctuate with market conditions. Obviously, as a borrower, your job is to figure out which type will give you the lowest rate over the entire term of the mortgage.

   The general rule of thumb is that a fixed rate mortgage would be best for you if it is under 10%. If the fixed rate quoted to you is over the 10% level, then you should lean toward an adjustable rate. The reason for this rule is that historically, the 10% level has been a pivotal point for interest rates. In most cases, if you make the decision to go with an adjustable rate when rates are over 10%, there is a better likelihood that interest rates will decrease rather than increase. Likewise, when rates are below 10%, there is a greater likelihood that they will rise, so you are better off locking in a fixed rate loan.

2. The length of your mortgage is a big consideration for long-term interest savings. For years, the standard conventional rate mortgage has been 30 years. People realized that shorter periods of time meant higher payments. Rarely, however, did anyone calculate the opportune length of a mortgage as compared to reasonable payment amounts. A better length of time seems to be 15 years instead of 30. But it would appear that paying off your mortgage in half the time would mean double payments. In reality, the payments do not double.

A chart of mortgage terms will show you that a $50,000 mortgage amount borrowed at 12% interest for 15 years requires a payment of $600 per month. The same mortgage, $50,000 on a 30-year schedule, requires a payment of $514 per month. While the difference between the two is only $86, you would have avoided 15 more years of payments at $514 per month and achieved a savings of $92,520.

Business Financing

The final area of financing to discuss is your business. The key here is debt burden. The prevailing business philosophy in America has been that bigger is better.

Consequently, businesses find themselves in the constant spiral of expansion, and expansion takes money. While it would be nice to think that this expansion could be covered by internal capital, most frequently debt is used. Once a company borrows money, it must produce more to pay on the higher debt, and it then needs to borrow more to expand in order to produce more--a vicious cycle.

Ask yourself some very important and soul-searching questions. Why are you in business? If the answer is to build an empire, that's one thing. If the answer is to make money to reach your goal, then the next logical question is "How much is enough?" I suspect many companies would find themselves more profitable and less stressful if they concentrated on maximizing the market they have instead of borrowing to try for more.

Recommended Study: If you are currently facing a credit problem or want to know more about dealing with creditors, we recommend *The Credit Pack,* by James L. Paris and Pearl Polto.

To order a copy of this book, please phone our resource center at 1-800-333-3700.

PRINCIPLE 4

THE POWER PRINCIPLE OF
HOME OWNERSHIP

Over our years of working with financial-planning clients around the country, we have found no other single investment that has proved to be so universally successful as the single-family home.

The American Dream is composed of many items. Probably the most sought after is home ownership. There is just something special about having a place that is yours and owning the ground underneath it. Unfortunately, however, this once easy-to-achieve goal is now a difficult challenge for many. The average home in America is now selling for over $100,000, and that's not the entire story. If you happen to live in an area like San Francisco, Los Angeles, or many parts of the Northeast, this modest figure can easily jump to $250,000 or more! Again, we are still just talking about a single-family home.

After working with thousands of individuals across the country attempting to buy their first home, we have developed the following four Power Principles:

1. Power of Assumable Mortgages

2. Power of Owner Financing

3. Power of Phone Qualifying

4. Power of Negotiating

Power of Assumable Mortgages

One of the most common myths today about home purchases is that an individual must have outstanding credit to become a home owner. Although outstanding credit is a plus, it is not a prerequisite to buying a home. As with most challenges, if something doesn't work one way, then try another approach; essentially, "where there's a will there's a way." This means that if your goal is the purchase of a home, don't give up if you are turned down for a mortgage. The true achiever views this simply as a temporary setback. So what is the easiest alternative?

The most common types of assumable mortgages are FHA or VA guaranteed mortgages. Many times a property owner may actually advertise the fact that the property has an assumable mortgage. Assumable mortgages can be assumed two ways: with qualifying and without qualifying. If the loan is assumable with qualifying, it is probably something that is not worth pursuing, since you may have already determined that you do not have the "ability to qualify." If the loan is assumable without qualifying, this means that regardless of your credit history, employment status, or any other criteria, you can fully assume the loan. Needless to say, many people in America are unaware of the existence of "non-qualifying" assumable mortgages.

The Power of Owner Financing

Another creative technique to finance the purchase of a home is the use of owner financing. Many individuals who have experienced difficulty in selling their property will resort to some form of seller financing as a means to expedite the sale of their home. In general, there are two basic approaches to this:

1. **Seller-Financed Second Mortgage**

In this scenario there is an assumable first mortgage, but a considerable difference between the sale price and the mortgage balance. This "equity" is the problem for the buyer. Let's look at an example:

$100,000   Asking price

$75,000   Assumable first mortgage

$25,000   Equity

In this transaction the buyer can attempt to negotiate for seller financing to cover the $25,000 in equity. Many times these "seller-take-back mortgages" are five-year loans with a balloon payment that is due at the end of the term. What typically happens is the buyer will acquire new financing before the lump sum payoff is due.

2. **Seller-Financed First Mortgage**

Believe it or not, some people actually own their home outright and have no mortgage. These people are usually retired and may be planning to sell their home and use the proceeds to purchase something much smaller and easier to maintain or to move into an assisted living center. When you find this situation, a creative buyer should be able to present a convincing case for this seller to finance a large percentage--or perhaps all--of this purchase.

Two reasons why:

1. Provides for a quick sale.
2. Creates an investment program with monthly income for the seller.

The motivation for a seller to enter into this arrangement (beyond the quick sale of their property) is an attractive investment opportunity. Remember, most retired individuals who sell their property will simply invest the money in CDs or money markets. By financing the sale of their own home, they can receive a secure monthly income stream at an interest rate much more attractive than other typical fixed income options. What safer security could an investor ever want than his own property?

The key to the above two approaches is that you must ask! Although you may feel very inhibited about proposing such arrangements, these types of deals are worked out each day all over the country. Remember, the worst thing they can say is no.

Power of Phone Qualifying

In his book *Nothing Down*, Robert Allen gives a stellar presentation on this subject. Read it if you can. The concept is simple: "Let your fingers do the walking."

Assuming that you are going to be a prudent shopper, you should really plan to look at fifty or more houses before you make a purchase. The key to your search is the telephone. Here is how it works: Make a list of all your "musts," and pre-qualify each property before you visit.

Example "must" list

· 3 bedrooms/2 baths

· 2000 sq. ft. +

· Assumable mortgage without qualifying

· Low down payment

This may sound extremely simplistic; however, you would be amazed at how many times people will use up valuable time driving to properties they would never buy or be able to buy.

Power of Negotiating

As the old saying goes, "everything is negotiable." A good friend of ours uses as his motto the saying "You don't ask, you don't know." What is the secret to negotiating? In his book *Negotiating Tactics*, Edward Levin places a great deal of emphasis on being a good listener. What does listening have to do with negotiating, you might ask? Unless you really understand the person you are negotiating with, you most likely will not be successful in your negotiations. Successful negotiations can really be summed up in this way: "getting your way by creatively allowing others to have their way." The oldest variation of this is the term P.S., price scenario. This is very common in everything from real estate to negotiating professional athletes' contracts. One party is allowed latitude in determining price while the other side determines terms (i.e., owner financing, length of contracts, closing date, etc.).

In his book *See You at the Top*, Zig Ziglar has probably put it best with his recipe for success in life: "The way to get what you want is by helping others get what they want." Well put.

Recommended Precautions

1. Have an attorney represent you at closing instead of using a neutral party to handle the closing.

2. Make your purchase contingent upon a satisfactory inspection by a certified property inspector.

3. Always buy title insurance and have a survey done.

Home ownership can be among the most rewarding experiences of the American Dream. You and your family will enjoy for years the ownership of your new home.

PRINCIPLE 5

THE POWER PRINCIPLE
OF TAX REDUCTION

All the way back to the days of Caesar and his "tax collectors," the idea of paying taxes has not set well with the average person. It is estimated that the average American now works each year until mid-May just to pay his taxes for the year. The Power Principle of Tax Reduction can undoubtedly change your financial future.

"Anyone may so arrange his affairs that his taxes shall be as low as possible. He is not bound to choose a pattern that will best pay the treasury."

--Judge Learned Hand

The Four Power Principles of Tax Reduction

1. Always Itemize

2. Increase Your Paycheck

3. Maximize Your Deductions

4. When Possible, Make Tax-Advantaged Investments

Always Itemize

One of the most common mistakes made in America is to choose the standard deduction instead of itemizing. Simply stated, the federal government gives you the choice as a taxpayer to either claim your specific tax deductions or opt for a "standard" deduction amount. Needless to say, this standard deduction does not provide very much in the way of total tax savings. The goal of all taxpayers should be to always have enough deductions to itemize.

Increase Your Paycheck

Most people in America are overpaying their taxes on each and every paycheck. Many individuals are not receiving the take-home pay they are entitled to. This overpayment is refunded the following year after the filing of their tax return. Think about that--we are losing the use of several hundred and in some cases thousands of dollars each year by having too much money withheld from our paychecks. What can we do about it? Federal law requires that employers must have their employees complete a W-4 form. We are responsible for choosing the number of "allowances" on our W-4. This information is then used to calculate our withholding.

Remember, an allowance is not the same as a personal exemption. This is where many people get confused. They elect the same number of allowances as personal exemptions. If you are getting a refund every year, you have too few allowances on your W-4 form. The reverse is also true: If you find yourself owing large amounts of money each year, you are taking too many withholding allowances. Remember, in an ideal scenario, you want to pay only that amount out of each paycheck that you will really owe. If you pay less than 90% of the taxes owed in a given year, you will be subject to IRS penalties. If you have determined that you are having too much withheld from your paycheck, request a new W-4 form and make the necessary adjustments by increasing allowances by one for every $650 you have been overpaying in taxes.

Maximize Your Deductions

The primary reason the average individual is not taking full benefit of all their possible deductions is lack of knowledge. The ironic thing, however, is that the IRS has literally hundreds of free publications available for the asking. For further information on this, call the IRS Publications Hotline at 1-800-829-3676. Another valuable IRS service is Teletax, which can be reached at 1-800-829-4477. This service allows you to choose a topic of interest and plays an audiotape message regarding that subject and the tax law. Also, the IRS conducts various free classes throughout the year in many parts of the country. For more information, call 1-800-829-1040.

When Possible, Make Tax-Advantaged Investments

As we discussed in Chapter 3, compound interest is one of the most dynamic power principles available to the average American. There is, however, one principle that can be even more powerful: compound tax-deferred interest. The easiest way to explain tax deferral is to consider it an interest-free loan from the government. That's right! The government gives taxpayers the choice of whether they want to pay taxes on their investment earnings each year or delay paying those taxes until a future date. Imagine someone loaning you money and offering to let you keep it for forty to fifty years interest free. That would be great, wouldn't it? The reality is that the government is affording us this opportunity every day of the year.

Let's look at the options:

IRA's, 401k's, 403b's, Keogh's, SEP IRA's, annuities, and other qualified plans are included in the category of tax-deferred investments. Among these there are two basic types:

1. Qualified
2. Non-Qualified

Qualified Plans

Qualified plans include such accounts as IRA's, 401k's, 403b's, SEP IRA's, defined benefit plans, profit sharing, etc. The commonality of these accounts is that they provide for both tax deferred growth and a tax deduction. This literally means that your earnings, if deposited into one of these accounts, will not be taxed as income until the money is withdrawn, nor will your deposit be taxed each year as it grows. Always maximize these plans first, before contributing to non-qualified plans.

Non-Qualified Plans

Although there are varying types, the most common is the annuity. The non-qualified plan allows your contributions to grow, tax deferred, but does not provide a tax deduction for the deposit of these funds. Consider this fact, however. If your tax-deferred investment is earning 10% a year, it will double four times in a 24-year period. This same rate of return on a fully taxable basis would only double three times in 24 years. Imagine that! Earning the same rate of return and having double the amount of money, that's a power principle!

Additional benefits of annuities:

- No maximum contribution limits
- No mandatory withdrawal at age 70 1/2 (as with IRAs)
- Creditor-proof in many states
- Unlimited switching between investments with no transaction fees
- No initial sales charges

As an average American, you are paying 20%-30% of every dollar you make in taxes. Employing our "Power Principles" can make a substantial impact on your future net worth. In the immortal words of Will Rogers, "There are only two things a man cannot avoid, death and taxes. When Congress meets each year, however, death does not get any worse." Although he is partially right, we cannot totally avoid paying taxes, but we can certainly reduce the amount we pay.

Recommended Study: For more information on annuities, we recommend the single cassette tape program *The Best Investment in America*. For more information on how to put your tax life in order, we recommend *The 30-Day Quick Start to Tax Freedom*.

To order, call our resource center at 1-800-333-3700.

PRINCIPLE 6

THE POWER PRINCIPLE
OF MONEY MANAGEMENT

During our lifetime we will literally have hundreds of thousands and, in many cases, millions of dollars pass through our hands. Most of us, unfortunately, will have little to show for it at retirement. As Andrew Carnegie said, "The problem of our age is the administration of wealth."

We as Americans have an unparalleled opportunity to accumulate fortunes during our lifetime, regardless of our situation. In this chapter we will discuss the driving force in the world--money. Money does not come with an instruction manual, but perhaps the following pages can serve as that. Once mastered, the "Power Principle of Money Management" can change your life.

The Four Power Principles of Money Management:

1. Pay Yourself First

2. 90% Is Enough

3. Control Your Cash Flow

4. Increase Your Income

Pay Yourself First

This simple yet powerful concept is not being used by many people. The principle is simple: Whenever you receive a check from your employer or proceeds from your business, make the first payment to yourself. We as Americans are very much in a "payment mode." The problem we have is never having enough left over to save for our future and, in many cases, not even enough to pay our current obligations. A client once put it well by saying that "There is always too much month at the end of the money." The habit of paying yourself first literally starts when you make the same, or actually greater, commitment to yourself than you make to your creditors. This is not a recommendation to stop paying your bills, but to start paying yourself. The average American budget goes something like this:

Once a month, take out all the "bills" and pay them. Whatever is left over is available for discretionary spending.

Do you see the problem here? If saving for retirement or your children's education is not included as a "bill," it will never get accomplished. Paying yourself first is an integral part of becoming financially independent.

90% Is Enough

Never spend more than 90% of your income. The remaining 10% should be allocated to investments. One surefire way to accomplish this is to enter your paycheck deposits for 90% of their total. For example, if you receive a paycheck for $500, simply enter this in your checkbook as $450. Next, set up an automatic check draft from your account for $50 every payday. An automatic draft will electronically transfer your funds to the mutual fund or other investment of your choice.

Recommended mutual funds for electronic deposit:

Financial Funds	1-800-525-8085
Twentieth Century	1-800-345-2021
Fidelity	1-800-544-6666
Vanguard	1-800-662-7447

These companies will supply you with the necessary paperwork to set up an electronic deposit.

We are strong believers in this strategy. The first time it became clear to me was after reviewing the portfolio of several clients whose employers offered automatic investment programs (such as mutual funds, government bonds, etc.). It was amazing to see how people of modest income could amass such great amounts of money. When asked how they had accomplished this, the common reply was "I never missed it--the money came right out of my paycheck." If your employer does not offer such a program, then the strategy outlined above is a very easy way to duplicate it. Remember, if you don't "have it," you can't spend it. We have yet to discover an income that could not be outspent. From individuals earning $20,000 to $200,000 and up, the problem is consistent--not enough money to keep up with their expenses, in most cases. Are you starting to see the lesson here? You must pay yourself first! Without employing this principle it will be nearly impossible for you to make a commitment to your future.

Control Your Cash Flow

In many cases, paying yourself first or even at all may not be possible because of mismanagement of funds. Budgeting is an absolute necessity in order for you to get control of your spending and your financial future. A budget is simply an itemized list of anticipated expenditures. The problem with budgeting is we frequently do not consider all of our needs when we budget.

A financial planner once told us that out of several hundred clients he had worked with over the years, none had ever included clothing as part of their budget. He went on to say that he noticed never once did a family come to his office naked. As humorous as this story seems, it teaches us a basic concept: Budgets should reflect all of our spending categories. If our budget is not accurate, it will most certainly be ineffective.

A basic budget should include:

- All fixed payments
- Household maintenance
- Automobile maintenance
- Clothing
- Food
- Entertainment and recreation
- Gasoline
- Utilities
- Insurance
- Savings and investments
- Child care costs
- Miscellaneous

Be sure that your budget is realistic. If it's not, you and your family will not stick with it. One of the most ingenious programs we have seen for budgeting is called the "envelope" system. How this works is simple. Every expense category is assigned an envelope, and the money for that category is put in that envelope.

As an example, if your budget allows for a $100 per month entertainment allowance, that envelope would start with $100. As the month progresses, use that money for entertainment. When the envelope is empty, you must stop using any money for entertainment. You may feel uncomfortable keeping cash around the house, so an alternative would be to keep slips of paper in envelopes to be used as a ledger to keep track of money spent from your checking account. An old Chinese proverb says that "If all the money in the world were divided equally between everyone, in a short period of time we would all be back right where we are." Think about it!

Increase Your Income

For many individuals, increasing their income may be a more realistic solution to overcoming their paycheck-to-paycheck struggles. While I could talk about this subject for hours, the idea of taking a part-time job or starting a small business is not that difficult. A retired couple I know has a booth at a local swap meet and averages $800-1,000 per weekend in profit! They started their business with less than $1,000 and earn $40,000 per year part-time.

Another idea is to become more valuable to your employer. That's right. What would it take for you to get a raise and promotion? If you don't know, ask. Schedule a meeting with your supervisor and ask him what you can do to become more valuable to the company. He may suggest education, specialized training, or other ideas to help you move up the corporate ladder. Contrary to

Contrary to popular belief, most managers are happy to help subordinates move up within the company.

Recommended Study: To get started quickly in a new small business, read *The 30-Day Business Quick Start.*

For information on how to order, call our resource center at 1-800-333-3700.

PRINCIPLE 7

THE POWER PRINCIPLE
OF PROTECTION

"The life insurance industry has become a voracious octopus squeezing the financial life's blood out of millions of American families."

--Arthur Milton

Protecting family, home, and possessions has always been one of man's goals. The instruments of protection have changed over the years. Now, for most of us, insurance does our protecting.

The subject of insurance is a sore spot with most people. Probably the most favorable thing people can say about insurance is that it's a "necessary evil." It seems like all our possessions and all activities we participate in are supposed to be insured, or so the insurance industry would like us to believe. In this chapter we will be dealing with various types of insurance, teaching you how to evaluate your need for coverage and the most economical way to purchase it.

The Four Basic Principles of Insurance:

1. Buy Only What You Need

2. Insure Your Life with Term Insurance

3. Protect Your Automobile and Yourself

4. Buy "Group" Health Insurance When Possible

Buy Only What You Need

Before we dive into the various categories of insurance, let's discuss insurance that should not be purchased.

1. Credit Life Insurance

This insurance is sold in conjunction with a loan. The basic concept is that if the borrower dies before the loan is paid off, the insurance company will cover the outstanding balance. That sounds pretty good, you might be thinking. Although it looks good on the surface, credit life insurance is nothing more than overpriced term insurance (which will be discussed later in this chapter). It is overpriced primarily because you pay the same amount per month for the insurance, even though your loan amount is decreasing. Our recommendation is to simply purchase an overall term insurance policy for the total protection you need and forget coverage on each loan.

2. Extended Warranties

This is also a form of insurance that sounds attractive but is overpriced and usually difficult to collect on. To give you an example, we recently purchased a $550 item from an electronics store. Before the cashier processed our purchase, we were hit with a sales pitch regarding an extended warranty. The cost was $100 for a year of unlimited service. Imagine that! I was being asked to pay nearly 20% of the value of the item to insure it against breakdown. To reiterate, the problem with these warranties is they are extremely overpriced. Decline extended warranties on all purchases from electronics to automobiles, for they are not a good value.

3. Credit Card Insurance

Insurance companies want to insure everything, including the credit cards in our wallets. Most credit card agreements put the cardholder at risk only up to a maximum of $50, and this is only if you have lost your card and not notified the company. Once you have notified the credit card company, in most cases you will have absolutely no liability. Don't waste your money on this insurance.

Three Areas of Insurance We Do Need

1. Life Insurance

If you are a frequent traveler, you will most likely notice, as we have, that the tallest buildings in most city centers seem to be those of insurance companies and banks. Life insurance companies have been reaping great profits over the last century because of consumer ignorance. As a rule, where most people go wrong in purchasing life insurance is in purchasing more "benefits" than they really need.

The two basic forms of life insurance are cash value and term insurance. Cash value policies, also referred to as whole life, allow your premiums to become an "investment" of sorts. What this means is that over a period of time you will have a buildup of value that you can withdraw, based on policy provisions.

Additionally, in whole life policies, this buildup of value is applied toward future insurance premiums. So, in essence, your insurance can become "paid up." This means that no more monthly premiums will be required. You may be thinking this sounds great, and it does!

The consumer can hardly resist this concept. The problem, however, is not uncovered until you look closer. According to Arthur Milton, author of *How Your Life Insurance Policies Rob You*, cash value insurance will cost you 8 to 10 times more than term insurance, and at some future date you may find that you have built up an equity of 25% of overpayment, which is not a good deal. It reminds me of a local golf course that frequently runs a special for a free round of golf. The only catch is that the cart fee is $25!

Most consumer-minded financial experts will recommend term insurance. This type of insurance provides nothing but death protection. If you die, the policy will pay off. That's no "bells and whistles." This insurance is sold far less frequently by insurance agents than cash value, the reason being commissions, of course.

2. Automobile Insurance

Automobile insurance is composed of two basic components: liability and collision. The liability portion of your auto insurance policy covers any damages you cause to other people

and their property. While most states set minimum requirements for liability, it is usually a wise decision to exceed them. As a rule of thumb, you should carry double your net worth in liability coverage. The second part of your auto insurance policy is collision. Collision covers any damages to yourself or your automobile. The additional feature of collision is called comprehensive. This covers theft, fire, vandalism, etc. If your automobile is valued at less than $2,000, it usually makes sense not to carry collision and comprehensive. The reason is obvious-- it would be cheaper to replace the automobile than to pay insurance premiums for any extended period of time.

One surefire way to save on your auto insurance is to increase your deductible to $500. This means you bear the risk for the first $500 in damages. This will usually substantially decrease your premiums. Many experts on the subject of auto insurance state that individuals with low deductibles are essentially overpaying to such an extreme that they could easily create an emergency fund from the decreased premium of a higher deductible. Therefore, they would become "self insured" for the deductible. In our experience, this is the case with most auto insurance companies.

The last step is to shop around. Insurance companies and rates on automobile coverage vary dramatically from city to city. For example, if you live in Miami, the most competitive insurer may be entirely different than the one you used in Des Moines, Iowa. That being said, we have found the following three companies to typically be the most competitive:

1. Geico
2. U.S.A.A.
3. State Farm

3. Health Insurance

We were intrigued on a recent trip to Canada when we were told that the tax on cigarettes was actually more than the cost of the cigarettes. The reason for this is that Canada has government-sponsored health care insurance. Since the government is at risk when you have health problems, they make their citizens pay dearly. The United States is also fast approaching a health care crisis. Ken Dychwald, author of *Age Wave*, says that the fastest growing segment of our population is the 85+ group. And, further, a typical American mom will now spend more years taking care of her parents than she will her children. The graying of America is just one of the factors contributing to the U.S. health care crisis.

What Can You Do?

If you are fortunate, your employer has provided a company-paid group health policy for you. If this is not the case, you will have to explore other options. "If you are not in a group, join a group," says Ralph Nader, author of *Winning the Insurance Game*. What this means is that to qualify for group health care rates, you may consider joining a trade association or national organization of some sort. Even after employing this strategy, you may want to carry a $1,000 deductible to save even more on your annual premiums. Regardless of what someone tells you, health insurance is a must. An additional option is to join the group plan of a working spouse. Ask the employee benefits office if this is possible. Many times it is and can save you a hefty sum on your premiums.

We have seen many people completely lose any chance of living the American Dream because of a poor insurance plan. By following the principles in this chapter, you will not be among them.

PRINCIPLE 8

THE POWER PRINCIPLE
OF INVESTING

To reach your American Dream, you must invest your money and then use it toward accomplishing your goals. Notice we said *use the money*. Idle money does no one any good.

The Four Power Principles of Investing

1. Develop a Plan

2. Start Early

3. Invest in What You Know

4. Don't Put All Your Eggs in One Basket

Develop a Plan

Almost no one has a plan when it comes to investing. Instead they invest in the current vogue investment, and usually by the time the average American learns about an investment it is already turning downward.

What we recommend is that you have a defined investment plan and stick with it. For some of you, the best investment will be in yourself or in your own business. In most cases, though, we will need a third party investment. To fill this need, we recommend no-load (no commissioned) mutual funds.

Why We Are Recommending Mutual Funds

Mutual funds are one of the easiest ways to start an investment program that you can grow with, in terms of both money and sophistication.

Some of the important advantages are:

1. **Professional Management.** Some of the brightest money managers in the country will be managing your mutual fund. Until you feel more comfortable making your own selection, doesn't it make sense to let professionals handle it for you?

2. **Diversification.** This is the cornerstone of the mutual fund philosophy. Instead of buying a single stock, an investment in a mutual fund gives you part ownership in a group of stocks. This allows even the beginning investor to diversify his portfolio and his risk.

3. **Lower Investment Cost.** Normally the small investor is at the bottom of the totem pole when it comes to clout. Small investors usually pay the highest fees and get the poorest service. By combining with other similarly minded investors, you form a powerful cooperative.

4. **Liquidity.** Access to your money can be extremely important in case of emergency. This is particularly true for the smaller investor. Mutual funds offer access to your cash in many ways, including simply writing a check out of one of your investments.

5. **Reinvestment of Dividends.** When you own stock, dividends are sent directly to you, the shareholder. Frequently, you cannot

simply reinvest the small dividend. Mutual funds allow you to invest all dividends or capital gains earned, no matter how small and without the transaction cost. Because of their automatic reinvestment, you can have the tremendous power of compounding working for you.

6. Timing. No investment vehicle is right for all economic markets. Mutual funds allow you to switch investments from stocks to bonds or to money markets instantly. This timing opportunity allows you to always have your money working for you where it will produce the highest return.

Some disadvantages of mutual funds include:

1. You can lose your money. Not all mutual funds are alike. Some are more aggressive than others. A mutual fund family such as Financial Funds will have a selection of conservative, moderate, and aggressive funds. However, remember the fund family is based on stocks and bonds, and although diversification helps you in case of disaster, you will be affected by market fluctuation.

2. They aren't totally management free. Because mutual funds do go up and down in value, you will want to keep an eye on your investment.

3. You do pay a management fee. The fee is really very small compared to all the advantages you get, and it's obvious the person managing your money must get paid somehow. Just make sure it's reasonable and in line with what other firms charge (usually from .5-3%).

Start Early

An investment plan is successful if it is continuous over a long period of time. Remember the importance of the 10% Solution and the miracle of compounding that we have previously discussed. Combine these with your investment plan for true success.

Invest in What You Know

Time and time again, people lose money in the get-rich-quick schemes that they never should have been involved with in the first place. Invest your money in what you know. This is one of the reasons we recommend mutual funds. The investment isn't complicated, and capable parties are available to manage it.

By now you know you don't need a "big hit" to reach your dreams and be successful, so why take the risk? Additionally, for most people it isn't even the monetary loss that is so bad. The real loss experienced in get-rich-quick schemes is the psychological one. The loss is frequently treated as some personal failure, and the defeat permeates other areas of the individual's life.

Don't Put All Your Eggs in One Basket

We have talked about the law of time change. Everything has a season, and what looks great today may not tomorrow. Likewise, investments change, and you should diversify so that change does not affect all your holdings. Diversification is also one of the very reasons we have recommended mutual funds as one of the ways for you to develop your plan.

Recommended Study: For more information on how to
                              invest in mutual funds, we recom-
                              mend the *30-Day Quick Start to
                              Mutual Fund Investing.*

                              To order, call our resource center at
                              1-800-333-3700.

PRINCIPLE 9

THE POWER PRINCIPLE
OF WORK

There are many thrilling moments in life. Among the very best of those times are when you get married, the birth of your children, and the day you take in the first dollar from your small business. Many people have framed that first dollar as a symbol of all that it represents. In this age of capitalism's rebirth, more and more people are turning to entrepreneurism. To some it is a necessity, to others a freedom of expression that goes to the fiber of our national heritage.

Important Note: To most people the term *entrepreneurism* is synonymous with having your own business. Instead, it should represent the spirit of accomplishment in your work. You can be your own boss and still be an employee in a company. It is only how you view the relationship and the job that's important.

The Five Power Principles of Work Are:

1. Do What You Like to Do

2. Get More Out of It Than Money

3. Don't Forget the Money

4. It Ain't Over 'Till It's Over

5. Start a Small Business

Do What You Like to Do

For however long we are here on this earth, we can choose to either enjoy it or be miserable. Since most of our waking time is

spent in some sort of work, it naturally makes sense that if we want
to enjoy life, we had better enjoy our work.

Some people say that they are not free to choose what they are
doing. These people frequently feel that they are where they are
because of facts and circumstances and that there is nothing they can
do about it. We totally disagree.

You are where you are today, doing what you are doing, because you chose for it to be that way. If you don't want it, then choose to change right now. Please understand that there will be consequences to every choice you make. Some of them may even be bad. The option, however, is yours.

That's all well, fine, and good, you may say, but it's me that will have to face the consequences. We understand. But if you are miserable doing what you are doing, what are you doing to yourself and your family, living the way you are? Note, again, we aren't saying use this as an excuse to leave your job tomorrow, but we are saying use this as the reason to plan a change as soon as you can.

Career Selection

Our schools spend a great deal of effort teaching us the history of our world and almost no time helping us understand what we as individuals are best at and what we should do with our life. If you like teaching and are good at it, doesn't it make infinitely more sense to spend a happy life doing what you like and are best at instead of doing something else that may even seem more prestigious and financially rewarding?

Fortunately, we live in a country that gives second, third, and fourth chances. Sometimes it even takes that long to find what you like. Just make sure you keep looking till you do. You are never too old or too anything that you can't launch that business you always wanted. Ray Kroc (McDonalds) and Colonel Harlan Sanders (Kentucky Fried Chicken) were both over fifty before they found their dream. The spirit of entrepreneurism is alive and well in America, and with the recent changes in the Soviet Union and Eastern Bloc countries, it will spread.

Get More Out of It Than Money

There will be a time in your life when money isn't everything. That time may not be now. For you, money may appear to be the most important thing in life, and we understand the feeling. But take our word for it--plan to also get something more than money, whatever you decide to do. If you don't, when the money comes, it won't be enough. What you do must fill your thoughts with passion. You must be able to feel the reward physically as well as mentally of a hard day spent. Ideally, your work should be a mission, part of what you want to accomplish throughout your life.

Don't Forget the Money

We want you to know that we realize that one of your rewards will be money. We do not believe that money is the root of all evil. We do believe that the love of money, to the exclusion of others, is. Therefore, one of the main keys to achieving the American Dream is to discover the work you like to do and figure out how to get someone to pay you enough money to get what you need.

It Ain't Over 'Till It's Over

In recent years this line, attributed to Yogi Berra, has been used in sports to demonstrate the philosophy of never giving up. Until the game is over, it is never too late to win. We believe that is also equally true as it applies to your work. It is never too late to change your career or profession. You are only given one life and only so much time. If for any reason it isn't going right, you can change.

Start a Small Business

Last, but certainly not least, consider starting a small business. As you are probably well aware, individuals who own businesses generally pay less in taxes on a percentage basis than does the "working class" employee. By starting a small business, you become instantly eligible for 27 legal tax deductions not available to you normally. Most of our clients have chosen to convert their hobby into a business--such as avid golfers teaching golf lessons, craft and antique fanatics selling their products, and fishing enthusiasts running weekend charters. The IRS has a free publication outlining the tax deductions that will be available to you as a small business owner. To request it, call 1-800-829-3676 and ask for publication #334.

Recommended Study:

For more information on how to start your own small business, we recommend *The 30-Day Business Quick Start.*

To order, call our resource center at 1-800-333-3700, ext. 3901.

PRINCIPLE 10

THE POWER PRINCIPLE
OF PERSONAL INDEPENDENCE

Some people speak of retirement as though it were a place in time. "When I reach retirement," these people say, "I am going to play golf (or whatever) all day."

Some people think of retirement as an attitude. "When I retire, I'm going to enjoy the good life," they tell their friends.

What both of these statements are suggesting is a desire to become independent at some point in life and do the things you want to do. Unfortunately, this way of thinking requires some future life-style change that frankly doesn't happen overnight or without proper planning. To reach the "state of retirement" (or independence) that most dream of will require you to plant seeds of success today that can be reaped tomorrow.

1. Plan for Your Financial Retirement

2. Plan for Your Retirement Work

3. Plan for Your Retirement Health

4. Enjoy It When You Are There

Plan for Your Financial Retirement

Everyone realizes that to retire in the manner they dream will require the accumulation of money or assets that produce more money or assets. The mistake they frequently make, however, is the assumption that this amount is a huge dollar amount. When we ask clients how much they think they will need to have at retirement, the common response is $1,000,000, even though most have never seen a million dollars nor have any real idea how to amass that amount. The result of this unrealistic view is a failure to develop a plan that will lead them to their goal.

Although there is no surefire formula for retirement living, a good plan for most people is to create a system so that at retirement, your "investments" produce the same amount of income you make now from your work.

Now think about it. You've made about $40,000 per year for most of your life. You're entering retirement age. Your house is almost paid off. Your kids are all out of school. Your car payments are over. Couldn't you now do what you want to do with an income of $40,000 per year without working? If you've been making $60,000 per year for most of your life, couldn't you now do what you want to do under these same circumstances with $60,000 per year coming from your investments?

The answer, of course, is yes. Oh, you might want to have a little more, and if you do, you work a little. You'd probably enjoy it. The key is to understand that your goal should be to create a 100% lifetime income from your investments. In other words, in your early years you worked for money, and now it works for you. Let's look at how this dramatic new idea works for your retirement independence.

John and Sally are both forty years old. They have two children, ages thirteen and eight. John and Sally both have good jobs. John makes $35,000 and Sally $22,000, or $57,000 per year combined.

The traditional approach for financial planning would be to ask John and Sally how much they want to have at retirement and for fundamental college plans. The college goals are easily definable, because we can calculate with relative certainty the cost of college for both kids and then plan an investment goal to reach that destination. The bigger problem with John and Sally is the answer to the question of how much they want at retirement. The answer is everything. I want the big lottery. Unfortunately, this throws out any realistic planning.

What if this were the question?

John, Sally, let's imagine 25 years from now. You're both sixty-five. Assume that were today. Your kids are grown. Your house is now paid off. If someone gave you $57,000 per year to live on, would you live comfortably and do what you want to do?

Answer? Of course!

And it's true. I realize some of you will want more. That's fine, because you can plan for it. But what we are looking at is finding a plan to follow.

Let's explore further.

Plan for Your Retirement Work

We know that retirement is supposed to mean that you have stopped working. However, if you followed our principles of work, work isn't work, so why retire from it? Instead, think about how you can change your role. Rather than being on the front line, teach others what you know. This could be true for tradespeople or company presidents. If you haven't always followed our principles of work, use your retirement as the launching point for doing what you have always wanted to do.

Retirement does not mean that we must stop living our dreams or following our passions. In fact, those are the very things we should do. So many fine people have died or gotten sick right after retirement. While we can't prove it, we strongly feel it is because traditional retirement takes away the focus of life.

Plan for Your Retirement Health

So far in this book, we haven't addressed one of the most important things in life, which is your health. No matter how much money you have or how much you have accomplished, if you don't have your health, you don't have much.

To enjoy retirement, we must be healthy. It is clear that sometimes there are events that affect our health no matter what we do. It is equally clear that there are things that we can do to help improve our health no matter what else happens.

We have listened and read widely to see what simple secret we could bestow to you on the subject of health. Interestingly, one word continues to come forward: moderation.

Eat moderately, drink moderately, exercise moderately, and your body will run well. Sorry, we cannot recommend that you smoke moderately.

Enjoy It When You Are There

We personally feel fortunate that we have observed people who have retired with passion. They have gained the wisdom of life's secrets and are enjoying its fruits. If you don't personally know people who are "there," look around you until you find them. Ask them what they do to enjoy "it" so much, and see if you can model their actions. Don't worry, these people will be happy to talk with you. They are retired, you see; they have found their American Dream.

Recommended Study: *Estate Planning for the 90's* (audiotape).

To order, call our resource center at 1-800-333-3700.

AFTERWORD

TO PART I

You have just completed the first step in your quest for the American Dream. It is a continual process of obtainment.

As you move along your road to achievement, you will need more help. In various places we have recommended additional books and tapes that we think will help you. In addition, we have established an entire research center. The J.W. Dicks Research Institute, Inc. is dedicated to helping you and people like you reach your dreams.

To find out more about the institute, phone us at 1-800-333-3700. Tell us that you want to join the team--The American Dream Team. Your admission is your dreams! Welcome!

PART II

QUESTIONS

&

ANSWERS

QUESTIONS & ANSWERS

INTRODUCTION

Each Saturday, from 3:00 to 6:00 p.m. EST, we present *The Jim Paris Show*, on radio, throughout the country. The program is a live, phone-in talk show that gives you, our listeners, a chance to get your questions answered.

In this next section of the book, we have repeated some of our most frequently asked questions and have given you our best answers.

We hope you find them helpful.

CONSUMER LAW

1. **I am always hearing people recommending small claims court to resolve disputes with retail establishments. Is this a good idea?**

Absolutely. Small claims court is designed for this very purpose. The term "small claims" literally means that the amount of damages being sued for is limited to a small amount. Depending on the state, it is usually less than $5,000. In most cases you do not need an attorney and the costs will usually be under $100. Many states do not allow attorney representation in small claims court. Essentially, it is two people having a discussion with a judge, similar to television's popular *People's Court*. Small claims court can be the leverage you need to recover your losses from a disreputable retailer.

2. **What can I do if I have been defrauded by a mail order company?**

If you want attention, call a regulator! In the case of mail order fraud, one of two federal agencies may take action on your behalf:

Postal Inspection Service
1-800-654-8896

Federal Trade Commission
Bureau of Consumer Protection
1-202-326-3128

The above organizations can be instrumental in recovering a loss. In addition, contact your State Attorney General's Office, which can refer you to the proper state agency for assistance.

3.   The auto dealership where I purchased my car refuses to honor my warranty. What can I do?

If you are having a difficult time resolving a dispute, go first to the dealership manager and attempt to work it out. Beyond that, you should go to a corporate or "zone" manager. If this does not resolve the issue, contact your state Consumer Protection Office or Attorney General. Many states are now enacting "lemon laws" to give consumers some ammunition to use against car dealers.

4.   I received a product through the mail that I did not order. The company is demanding payment. What are my rights?

Simply write on the box "Merchandise not ordered" and drop it off at the post office. It will then be forwarded back to the company. If the harassment continues, contact the Postal Inspection Service mentioned previously.

5.   My company refuses to release the amount of pension benefits I am entitled to, even though I resigned over two years ago. Is there anything that can be done?

File a complaint with:

Pension and Welfare Benefits Administration
U.S. Department of Labor
1-202-219-8784

In addition, we would advise filing a complaint with the Internal Revenue Service, which would be very interested in any improper use of funds. The threat of filing this kind of complaint is also very intimidating to an employer, because if he hasn't paid you, he has probably done other things he doesn't want the IRS to discover. You may find a quick road to settlement.

6. My attorney has not acted in good faith in handling a legal matter, and I feel this has cost me a considerable amount of money. To whom can I complain?

Contact the Attorney Grievances Department of your state bar association. They will investigate and offer arbitration to resolve consumer losses resulting from careless attorneys.

7. On a recent airline trip, my luggage was damaged. After I reported this to the airline, they refused to compensate me for this loss. What can I do?

Complaints regarding airlines can be made to:

U.S. Department of Transportation
Office of Consumer Affairs
1-202-366-2220

8. My bank rolled over my CD without permission and now refuses to correct the error. In order to get my money, I must pay a six-month interest penalty. What do you recommend I do?

The bank will first try to tell you there is nothing they can do. They are lying. They can totally reverse the transaction. Don't waste time with a teller; get with a bank officer. If they don't help, ask to see the president. If that doesn't help, tell them you intend to contact the local television station's Consumer Affairs Department and that you are contacting your state's Department of Banking and Finance.

9. **This past year I was scheduled to take a cruise, and the cruise line had to cancel it because of mechanical problems. I am now getting the runaround and cannot get a refund. What do you suggest?**

Contact:

Federal Maritime Commission
1-202-523-5807

You should also find out if the cruise line is a member of any trade association that may have an arbitration in its membership rules.

10. **My company refuses to pay me overtime and seems to be getting away with this practice with all the employees. What can we do?**

Contact:

Wage and Hour Division
U.S. Department of Labor
1-202-219-8727

This department of the government is a tough group on overtime. Not only will they follow up on your complaint, but if you are right, they will help you collect for back pay.

Remember the following steps in resolving a complaint:

1) Contact the company and allow it an opportunity to resolve the problem.

2) Contact the corporate headquarters of the company.

3) Make a complaint to the proper regulatory agency.

4) Use the court system as a last resort.

The most important aspect of this entire process is to put everything in writing. Send all your correspondence by registered mail, and keep copies of everything. If you ever need to go to arbitration or court, the amount of paperwork you have will add credibility to your case.

INVESTMENTS

1. **The 1990's offer the investor a confusing array of investment choices. Why do you especially like mutual funds over all the other possibilities?**

This is a frequent question, and the best answer comes from our experience with over 30,000 individuals over the past several years. Mutual funds, in our research, have provided more success to individual investors than any other investment area. We believe this is because of four reasons:

1) They are easy to understand.

2) They are completely liquid.

3) They have professional management.

4) They offer diversification.

Most other investment options do not provide all of these benefits to the investor.

2. **What is an annuity?**

An annuity is an investment contract between an individual and an insurance company. In the early 1900's, annuities were very limiting. Typically, the only option for the investor was a fixed account earning as little as four percent. The investment community has taken this concept and broadened it to include mutual fund choices as well as these fixed accounts. When an annuity offers mutual fund choices, it is known as a variable annuity. The term simply implies that the investment value of the account can fluctuate, hence the term "variable." Although there is a risk of loss in these variable accounts, they typically outperform their fixed rate counterparts. The relationship is similar to that between growth funds and CD's.

Another interesting point is the "separate account rule." This means that all funds in a variable account are not commingled with the general funds of the insurance companies. Essentially, what this means to the investor is that only when you are investing in a "fixed" annuity is your principal at risk as it relates to the financial condition of the insurance company. Remember, however, in a variable account your principal is subject to market risk.

3. **What is the real difference between "load funds" and "no-load funds"?**

Although there have been many rumors over the years stating that load funds do better than no-loads, these stories cannot be substantiated by fact. Therefore, we have concluded the only difference between load and no-load is the sales commission (load). Other claims that are made include the statement that load funds have lower expenses, but again this is not true. Although *some* load funds have lower expenses than *some* no-loads, in general, it is the same across the board. Remember, the sales commission does not go to the mutual fund company, but to the financial salesperson. Because of this fact, there is no direct correlation between sales charges and expenses. Most mutual fund companies charge approximately .5%-3% for total management services.

4.   What is a "family" of mutual funds?

The term "family" is used to describe a mutual fund company that offers numerous choices of funds within their company. The most simplistic version of this is the availability of a stock fund, bond fund, and money market fund. With the increasing choices made available, it is easily conceivable to have over 100 options in a mutual fund group. The many options include aggressive and/or conservative variations on stock and bond funds, as well as a variety of choices in the international realms. Additionally, many investors are now flocking to sector funds (see question 6 for more details on these funds).

5.   What is your opinion of international funds?

International funds, like all mutual funds, are appropriate in the right situation. However, we do not believe that everyone should own some international funds all the time. This position is being pushed primarily by the same crowd that is suggesting that all investors should own a little of everything to be "well diversified." We would argue that they will have diluted results since they may very well be overdiversified. An additional consideration is to be careful which international funds you are investing in. They are not all the same. For example, there are specific funds that invest in the Pacific Basin (Japan, Korea, etc.) and others that are European in flavor, while yet others invest specifically in South Africa. The point is not to just invest internationally, but to know specifically about what part of the world you are doing your investing in.

6. What is a "sector" mutual fund?

Sector mutual funds concentrate on one specific industry. Consequently, they are not as diversified as typical mutual funds. For example, if you believe that the health industry will do well, you can buy a health sector fund. Some of the other sectors available include medical, energy, retail, banking, broadcasting, computer, biotechnology, and many others. The best two sources for sector funds are Fidelity (1-800-544-6666) and the Financial Funds (1-800-525-8085).

7. How do interest rates affect the stock and bond markets?

Historically, the stock market has done well during times of low interest rates. This is primarily for two reasons:

1) Corporations can borrow money cheaply and therefore are more likely to expand their business and create more profits, which will increase their stock price.

2) Consumers, like corporations, can also borrow money more cheaply and will tend to spend more. Therefore, this increase in consumer spending will positively affect corporate earnings.

8. What is your opinion of options and futures contracts?

A good friend of ours says, "If you want to gamble, go to Las Vegas, because the girls are prettier." In our opinion, options and futures are as close to out-and-out gambling as you can get. The only reasonable use of options and/or futures is as a market hedge by a professional money manager. Although we could get into a complicated discussion of this, the best advice is to say no to options and futures brokers.

9. What system of market timing do you recommend for mutual fund investors?

We have looked at a variety of approaches, and the only one that seems to work consistently over the long term is called "moving averages." Moving averages are a form of technical analysis. The premise is that once a market establishes a trend, it will continue in that direction until major economic events occur. At this point, a new trend develops in another direction.

CREDIT

1. What is a credit report, and how difficult is it for an individual to get a copy of their personal report?

A credit report is an historical record of an individual's credit payment history. A simple way to remember this concept is by calling it a "payment report card." Anytime an individual is denied credit because of derogatory information derived from the credit bureau, they are entitled to a free copy of their credit report.

2. What are the major differences between Visa/Mastercard and American Express?

Visa and Mastercard accounts are easier to qualify for and are designed to allow an individual to carry a credit balance, usually at high interest rates. Cards like American Express, Diners Club, and Carte Blanche are called travel and entertainment cards. These cards require a higher annual income from cardholders and do not charge interest, since cardholders are required to pay off their balance in full each month.

3. Is there an easy way to get a credit card if you have little or no credit history?

The answer is yes, by getting a "secured credit card." These Visa/Mastercards look just like any other card, and the only difference is that the cardholder is required to make a bank deposit, which serves as collateral for the credit line.

For example, if you desire a $500 credit line, you would be required to deposit $500 in an escrow account at the issuing bank. Over time, if you make your payments promptly, you will become eligible for unsecured cards.   For further information on banks offering these programs, call our offices at 1-800-333-3700.

4.   With all the different credit cards available, I am confused about which to choose, since they all have differing annual fees and interest charges.

As a general rule, interest rate charges are a more important consideration for most people than the annual fee charge.   This would not be true, however, if you do not run a balance or run a very low balance.   In these cases it would be better to pay a lower annual fee in lieu of higher interest charges.   A simple way to determine this is to calculate the estimated net cost for a year of any given card before making your final decision.   Again, interest rate charges are usually a more important factor than an annual fee, but not always.

5.   What can I do if I find an incorrect charge on my credit card statement?

The Fair Credit Billing Act of 1975 allows you to dispute any incorrect billing information on your credit card statement.   Simply send the credit card company a letter explaining the error, and they will then investigate it with the merchant.   The burden of proof is on the *merchant*, not on you.   Additionally, you are not required to pay any amount that is placed in dispute until the matter is resolved.   This also applies to overcharges, defective merchandise received, etc. If you do not get cooperation from your credit card company, it may be necessary that you contact the Federal Trade Commission in Washington, D.C. This is the government agency that regulates these types of problems.

6. I have a common last name and am frequently denied credit because of incorrect information in my credit file. Is there anything I can do?

Unfortunately, this is a problem that is very common. As a matter of fact, about 10% of the people in our seminars say they have had incorrect data on their credit report at least once, and linked it to other individuals with a similar name. The only real solution is to check your credit file carefully before making application for a loan. One service is available that provides several free copies per year of your credit file. It is TRW Credit Credentials. Also, remember that anytime you are denied credit, you can receive a free copy of your credit report.

7. What is your opinion of charging products I purchase with a department store credit card?

This is not typically a good idea, and the reason is simple. Most department stores will gouge you with excessive interest rate charges. If you are planning to purchase an item on credit, it would be much better to arrange financing in advance at your bank or credit union to ensure the best interest rate. Remember, low interest rate credit cards are available--you just need to shop for them as you do for merchandise.

8. How long will my credit history follow me?

According to federal law, credit information is not to extend longer than seven years. There is one exception--bankruptcy. This can stay on file for up to ten years.

9. A relative has asked me to co-sign on a loan for them. What does this mean, and what is my potential liability?

A cosigner is typically in a position of secondary liability, which means if the borrower does not pay as arranged, you can be pursued for the deficiency. Remember, if you co-sign a loan, you may have to make the payments. If you are not financially able to make such a commitment, then we would recommend against it.

10. Is there anywhere I can go to get counseling on managing my debt?

Yes, the Consumer Credit Counseling Service (CCCS), a United Way agency, has offices in most cities and can provide useful assistance in debt consolidation counseling as well as negotiations with your creditors to assist you in avoiding bankruptcy.

REAL ESTATE

1. Does it ever make sense for an individual to rent instead of buy?

Yes, especially if you are new to a community and not sufficiently aware of the real estate market to make an educated decision. Many times we will recommend that an individual rent for six months to one year before actually buying a home in an unfamiliar community. Additionally, if you are uncertain that you will be living in the area for at least three to five years, buying may be a bad decision. While it obviously makes sense to buy your own home at some point in your life, individual circumstances may dictate otherwise.

2. What is your opinion of the late-night real estate gurus and the whole "nothing down" fad?

While we believe that most of the strategies taught are legitimate, there is a certain amount of caution to keep in mind. For example, while it may be easy to acquire ten to twelve properties over a one-year period with no money down, there are other considerations. Are you prepared and able to manage these properties? This includes rent collection, repairs, and many other tenant-related problems.

Do you have adequate cash reserves? Depending on your community and the location of your properties, you may have extended periods of vacancy. To prepare for this possibility, you should have adequate financial reserves. This is also true regarding major repairs such as re-roofing, etc.

Again, these real estate strategists do have some great ideas. If they are guilty of anything, it is not telling individuals about the negative side of owning real estate. We assure you, as would any other real estate investor, that it is not all fun and profits.

3.   **When does it make sense to pay off a home mortgage? I have been told it should never be done, since the interest is tax deductible.**

This is definitely a frequent question we are asked, and the answer is *it depends*. Let's start by analyzing the "tax benefit" of keeping your mortgage.

10.0%	Interest Rate
- 2.8%	Tax Deduction (assuming 28% tax bracket)
7.2%	Net Cost of Interest

Once you determine the "net cost" after the tax deduction of your mortgage interest, the decision is simple. Can you earn more by investing the money elsewhere and continuing the mortgage payment? The typical result of this calculation is that individuals younger than fifty may end up investing instead of paying off their mortgage early. Other individuals may not feel comfortable taking the risk it would involve to earn substantially more than the cost of keeping the mortgage.

4. I have been approached by an individual who is selling a bi-weekly mortgage system for $495.00. Is this a good deal?

No! While the idea of investing your payments is a good one, paying someone for the calculation isn't. Rather than paying these expensive fees, you can easily emulate this by adding the same amount once each year. The results are almost exactly the same.

5. How does an individual pay off a 30-year mortgage in 15 years?

The process is simple enough. All that is needed is a current copy of your amortization schedule. On this schedule you will see a column named "principal." Based on the payment number you are on, look across the schedule to determine what amount is principal instead of interest, and add this amount to your payment. By following this simple procedure every month, your payment period will be cut in half.

6. What are "points," and are they negotiable?

A point is equal to one percent of the amount of money you are borrowing. These points are usually the "commission" that is earned by the loan broker. Points *are* negotiable, as is any feature of a loan or a mortgage. We don't quite understand why, but most people will not attempt to bargain with banks and other lending institutions. The truth is that everything is negotiable, including points. It may in some cases be to your advantage to pay more in points to lock in a lower rate. This is especially true if you know you will own the property for the long term.

7. What is title insurance, and do I really need it?

Yes, yes, yes! Title insurance guarantees that you are receiving the property free and clear of any title defects. Imagine someone informing you six months after buying a property that they have a judgment against your property for $20,000 to $30,000! This can and does happen. Remember, as they relate to real estate, judgments are typically against the property and not the individual who owns it. Thus, if you buy a property with a lien against it, you are **stuck**. The only way to avoid against this is by transferring this risk to an insurance company. For a few hundred dollars you can obtain insurance that protects you against this ever happening. *Always* buy title insurance.

8. How does an individual invest in mortgages or what I hear called "discounted mortgages"?

Many people find it a very profitable exercise to become a "bank" and get involved in mortgages. Just as banks buy and sell mortgages because of the attractive interest rates and safety, many individuals are now flocking to this area. An interesting twist is called "discounted mortgages." In this scenario investors find individuals who own mortgages (perhaps they have sold a home and financed a portion of it) and persuade them to sell these mortgages at a discount to their full face value. For example, if an individual owns a $10,000 mortgage at 9%, he would collect approximately $125 per month for ten years. Suppose rather than collecting these payments he would agree to a lump sum of $7,000 from an investor.

Here is what would happen:

$7,000 Invested

$125 Monthly Payment

Yield to Investor: 18% Annually!

The best place to find discounted mortgage opportunities is at your county courthouse or by advertising. An ad that we have seen used effectively is:

"Have you sold your home and taken back a mortgage? I buy mortgages for cash.

Call Jim at xxx-xxxx."

9. **When should I lock in a fixed rate instead of using an adjustable rate mortgage?**

Historically, anytime you can get a 10% or lower rate, lock in!

10. How do I ensure that a home I am buying does not have structural problems?

Always make all purchase offers contingent on the satisfactory inspection of a certified property inspector. These individuals can be found through your yellow pages and will cost $150-200 for a full walk-through inspection.

INSURANCE

1. How much life insurance does a person need, and how is a sufficient amount determined?

This is the age-old question and obviously one that most insurance salesmen have a conflict of interest in answering. The reason is simple. The more insurance you purchase, the more they earn in commission. Over the years a good rule of thumb that has been used is to multiply your annual expenses by some factor between eight and ten. This allows the survivors to invest the death benefit, and by earning ten to twelve percent they can receive the income needed to cover household expenses.

2. Does a non-working spouse need to be covered by life insurance?

It depends. If there are children involved, the answer is a definite yes. If the services of the homemaker had to be replaced, the costs would be substantial. Imagine the expense of hiring some-one to attend to three children, clean the house, prepare the meals, and take care of a host of other activities. The working spouse would certainly not add this sixty-plus-hour-per-week burden to their schedule. The way to approach this is to determine what it would cost to replace these services in the home and again multiply by a factor of eight to ten. Therefore, the survivors could invest the death benefit and create an income stream that would cover these expenses.

3. Should I buy life insurance on my children?

No. The reason for life insurance is to replace the loss of an economic value. Most children are not income producing and thus are not candidates for life insurance. The only exception to this may be a small policy of five to ten thousand per child in order to cover burial expenses.

4. What amount of liability insurance should I carry on my automobile?

This is a great question. Again, as with most insurance questions, there is no standard answer. We suggest, however, that you carry approximately two times your net worth.

5. What is an "umbrella liability" policy, and is it a good idea?

This policy is designed to pay off in the event that you are sued for more than you are covered for by your automobile and homeowners liability coverage. Typically, an insurance company will only sell you this coverage if you have your home and auto coverage with them. Once you have met a required minimum on each of these policies, you can purchase an inexpensive umbrella liability policy. In many cases for less than $350 per year, a million dollars in additional liability coverage can be obtained. Remember, this does not cover liability stemming from any professional activities.

6. My parents are getting up in age and have accumulated a sizable estate. They are contemplating the purchase of a large insurance policy to cover the future estate taxes that will be due. Is this a good strategy?

The answer is a qualified maybe. For the most part, we could say that a person should not spend the last ten "golden years" of their life paying expensive insurance premiums in lieu of their life dreams such as travel, etc. We were amused recently seeing a bumper sticker on a large motor home that read "I am spending my children's inheritance." It is not always this simple, however. In the case of a family estate or business, these assets may have to be sold to pay estate taxes, and because of family sentimental value they may be paid through a life insurance policy.

7. What is your opinion of buying travel insurance at the airport?

This is without a doubt one of the worst insurance purchases you can make. The odds of dying in a plane crash are astronomically low. The real reason not to buy travel insurance at the airport is because most credit companies offer it free if you buy your tickets with their credit cards.

8. If I feel that I have been defrauded in an insurance transaction, what should I do?

1) Contact the manager or the salesperson that you are working with and explain the situation. Allow him a few days to rectify it.

2) If the problem is not resolved to your satisfaction, contact the corporate headquarters and allow them an opportunity to solve it.

3) As a last resort, contact your state's Department of Insurance and file a written complaint.

In most cases these problems are resolved at the company level.

9. My employer does not provide health insurance. What is the minimum type of coverage I need, and how can it be purchased inexpensively?

We would recommend major medical, which is designed for catastrophic illness coverage. No, it will not cover routine doctor's visits or eyeglasses, but it will cover long-term illnesses. If you are not in a group, form one or join one. Our pastor, for example, has health insurance through a trade organization for pastors. Whatever time and effort is involved, it is well worth it to find a way to buy your health insurance as a part of a group.

Recommended Study:

If you have learned from these questions and would like to hear more, order *The Best of the American Dream*, a cassette tape highlighting the best of our radio show, *The American Dream*, each month.

To order, call our resource center at 1-800-333-3700.

PART III

GLOSSARY

OF

TERMS

Adjustable Rate Mortgage

A mortgage agreement between a financial institution and an individual that allows for adjustments to the interest rates at specified intervals. These adjustments are usually tied to an index such as the interest rate on U.S. Treasury Bills or average mortgage rates nationally. The agreement usually provides for a "cap" or limit that the rate can increase, both annually and for the life of the loan. These loans are a good strategy when interest rates are high, since a lower initial rate can be acquired and later the loan can be converted or refinanced when overall rates are lower.

Agent

A representative; one who is authorized to act on behalf of another.

Amortization

Payment of a debt by regular installments.

Annuity

These investment vehicles are usually divided into two categories, fixed and variable. Fixed annuities provide a guaranteed rate of return for a fixed period of time. Variable annuities provide the opportunity for the investor to choose from various "portfolios." These portfolios are like mutual funds. Variable annuities usually are better investments for individuals investing for a long period of time. This is because they allow for participation in the stock, bond, or international markets, which have historically outpaced inflation.

Assumption of Mortgage

The taking over of an existing mortgage by a buyer.

Balanced Mutual Fund

A mutual fund that buys stocks, bonds, and money markets. These portfolios are known for providing for a higher degree of safety in exchange for lower overall returns. Individuals looking for higher returns are usually attracted to specific mutual funds (i.e., stock funds, bond funds, international funds, etc.). These funds allow for more concentrated results and require more active involvement since they are more sensitive to market fluctuations. Balanced mutual funds are a good alternative for individuals seeking a low level of involvement and greater stability in a variety of market conditions.

Balloon Mortgage

A form of financing that requires periodic payments and a final large (balloon) payment to satisfy the loan.

Bankruptcy

A state of insolvency of an individual or corporation. U.S. bank-ruptcy laws provide for the inability to repay debts. There are two primary forms of bankruptcy: Chapter 7--Liquidation and Chapter 11--Reorganization. The basic difference between these is that Chapter 7 does not provide for the repayment of creditors and usually involves the discharging of debt. Chapter 11 is a reorgan-ization involving creation of a plan to repay a debt. Some items that are typically negotiated are interest rate, payment period, and other terms of the loan agreement.

Bond

Also know as debenture, a bond is issued by a corporation or government. These debt instruments provide for a specific date of repayment (known as the maturity date) and for periodic interest payments. Corporate and municipal bonds are rated by Moody's. A Moody rating is an evaluation of the ability of the issuer to repay the debt. U.S. Treasury securities are not rated since they are backed by the U.S. government. The highest rating that can be issued by Moody's is AAA. Municipal bonds are free from state income tax (if the recipient of the interest payments is a resident of that state). U.S. Treasury securities are exempt from state and local income tax.

Buyer's Market

When the supply of available properties exceeds the demand.

Capital Gain

The positive difference between an asset's purchase price and its selling price. In the event that the sale price is lower than the purchase price, it is referred to as a "capital loss." As of 1986, capital gains are taxed at the same rate as regular income.

Certificate of Deposit

A debt instrument issued by a bank. CDs are usually available in a wide range of maturities, and in most cases are protected through FDIC depositor's insurance. The rates paid to the depositor vary based on economic conditions and competitiveness in the marketplace.

Collateral

An asset pledged as security to a lender until a debt is repaid. This is most common in the area of home mortgages and automobiles. Loans that do not require collateral are called "unsecured loans," common examples of which are credit cards and personal lines of credit.

Collectibles

Items purchased by specialized collectors. These items include coins, stamps, baseball cards, albums, photographs, and antiques. Although the buyers of these items perceive them as "investments," they typically make poor investments because of the mark-up from the dealer to the consumer. Additionally, risk is present because "fads" that create increases in the price of these objects are unpredictable. Most experts in the investment community would not recommend this area unless an individual has a high level of expertise.

Commodities Contracts

These speculative investments are often referred to as "Options on Futures" or "Futures." This investment area allows the investor to speculate on the future price of items such as grain, metal, oil, and various types of food, including citrus and coffee. Most individuals who invest in commodities are trying to hedge other existing investments. An example of this might be a citrus farmer who buys citrus futures so that if his crop does not yield a healthy harvest, his "put" contract may pay him a compensating profit. This helps individuals in various industries protect themselves against industry-wide problems such as citrus freezes. Because of the high degree of risk involved in these investments, they are not recommended for the novice.

Consumer Protection Act of 1968

Federal legislation that requires fair and proper disclosure from lender to consumer. Such details as annual percentage rate and special loan terms, among others, must be openly disclosed.

Credit Rating

An established record of the payment history of an individual or corporation. These records are retained by credit bureaus, which provide this information to its members to assist them in making an evaluation on the credit risk of a loan.

Equity

The difference between the amount of indebtedness and the market value of an asset. The term *equity* is typically referred to in relation to a home.

Estate Tax

Tax imposed on assets left to heirs in a will. Current tax laws allow for an exclusion from federal estate taxes on the first $600,000 of assets. Through the use of a trust, this amount can be increased to $1,200,000.

Fair Market Value

The price at which an asset can be readily sold.

General Lien

A claim that may affect all of the properties of a debtor.

Ginnie Mae

Nickname for Government National Mortgage Association. These mortgage-backed securities provide funds for banks to lend for home purchases. These are sometimes referred to as "pass through" securities, referring to the fact that a bank will make a loan and then sell it on the secondary market. This basically means that they are not funding the mortgage but merely creating the contract. One note of caution is that Ginnie Maes pay the investor monthly both principal and interest. This means that part of your monthly payment is the return of your original investment.

High Yield Bonds

Known as "junk bonds," these debt instruments are typically high yielding and low rated. Bonds rated BB or lower are referred to as "junk." Although these bonds are risky, they are sometimes recommended in mutual funds, where the diversification allows for a partial diffusing of this risk.

Inflation

The rise of cost in consumer goods and services.

Joint Tenancy

An estate or interest owned by more than one person, each having equal rights to possession and enjoyment.

Lease

A contract involving the rental of an asset. This can involve real estate, equipment, automobiles, etc.

Leverage

The use of borrowed funds to finance the purchase of an asset.

Loan to Value (LTV) Ratio

The ratio of a mortgage loan in relation to the value of the property.

Margin Account

An account that allows the investor to borrow funds from the brokerage firm in order to buy securities. Federal law restricts an individual from borrowing more than 50% of the purchase price of a security. Margin accounts are typically used in "bull markets," where the cost of borrowing can be easily exceeded because of increasing stock prices. This type of account is recommended only for aggressive, seasoned investors.

Mortgage Broker

One who finds a mortgage lender for a borrower.

National Association of Securities Dealers

A nonprofit organization that supervises the sales practices of broker/dealer firms in the United States.

Over Improvement

An addition or improvement to a property that causes the value of that property to exceed a reasonable future sales price and make the improvement recoverable.

Penny Stock

These are stocks that sell for less than one dollar per share. Penny stocks are usually new issues and are very risky but offer tremendous upside potential.

Prepayment Clause

A provision in a mortgage that allows the mortgagee to reduce the debt at an accelerated pace without penalty.

Second Mortgage

A loan that is junior to a first mortgage, normally taken out when the borrower needs more money.

Sector Fund

A specialized mutual fund that invests in a specific industry. Fund groups that have such funds available are Fidelity and Financial Funds. Some of these sectors are energy, retail, and biotechnology.

Securities and Exchange Commission

The federal agency set up to regulate the purchase and sale of securities in the United States.

Self-Directed IRA

An IRA account that allows an individual to make their own investment choices and allows for maximum flexibility of investment options.

Seller's Market

When the demand for available properties exceeds the supply.

Tax Credit

A dollar-for-dollar tax reduction.

Title Insurance

An insurance policy that protects the holder from any hidden claims against the property.

Uniform Gift to Minors Act

A federal law that allows for proper management of assets for the benefit of a minor until that minor reaches the age of majority.